Mastering Storyboarding

This book offers a comprehensive and practical introduction to the fundamentals of storyboarding, making it an ideal resource for aspiring filmmakers, animators, and visual storytellers. It bridges the gap between written scripts and visual storytelling by demonstrating how scenes are translated into storyboard panels. Readers can see how scripts are broken down into individual shots and how those shots are visually constructed on the page.

Each example includes detailed illustrations of storyboard panels that correspond to script excerpts, giving readers a clear sense of how to interpret narrative beats and visualize camera movement, composition, character blocking, and shot progression. This book explains key concepts in cinematic language—such as shot types (wide, close-up, over-the-shoulder, etc.), camera angles, and transitions—and shows how they are effectively employed in storyboarding.

By studying these examples, readers will gain a deeper understanding of the visual grammar of film. They'll learn not only how to recognize different shot types but also how to purposefully select and apply them to enhance storytelling, create emotion, and guide the viewer's eye.

Whether you're a student or a working professional looking to sharpen your skills, this book serves as both an instructional manual and an accessible visual reference guide.

Caroline Hu is a renowned character designer known for her work on several high-profile animated features and television shows. After graduating from CalArts, Caroline began her journey in character design and visual development at Disney, where she worked on films such as *Mulan, Dinosaur, The Lion King,* and *Fantasia 2000*. At Warner Bros., she worked on animated features such as *Quest for Camelot* and *Osmosis Jones*, for which she was the sole character designer. Her talent for creating unique and memorable characters quickly made her a sought-after artist in the industry. She is currently a professor of animation at several universities in Los Angeles and is also the author of *Mastering Character Design: Design with Intent and Purpose* with CRC Press. She lives in California with her family, her two smokin' hot rods, and her non-smokin' daily driver.

Mastering Storyboarding

Professional Techniques for Visual Storytelling

Caroline Hu

CRC Press
Taylor & Francis Group
Boca Raton London New York

CRC Press is an imprint of the
Taylor & Francis Group, an **informa** business

Designed cover image: Caroline Hu

First edition published 2026
by CRC Press
2385 NW Executive Center Drive, Suite 320, Boca Raton FL 33431

and by CRC Press
4 Park Square, Milton Park, Abingdon, Oxon, OX14 4RN

CRC Press is an imprint of Taylor & Francis Group, LLC

Library of Congress Cataloging-in-Publication Data
Names: Hu, Caroline author
Title: Mastering storyboarding : professional techniques for visual storytelling / Caroline Hu.
Description: First edition. | Boca Raton FL : CRC Press, 2026. | Includes index.
Identifiers: LCCN 2025032627 (print) | LCCN 2025032628 (ebook) |
ISBN 9781032985084 hardback | ISBN 9781032985077 paperback |
ISBN 9781003599036 ebook
Subjects: LCSH: Storyboards
Classification: LCC NC1002.S85 H83 2026 (print) | LCC NC1002.S85 (ebook)
LC record available at https://lccn.loc.gov/2025032627
LC ebook record available at https://lccn.loc.gov/2025032628

ISBN: 9781032985084 (hbk)
ISBN: 9781032985077 (pbk)
ISBN: 9781003599036 (ebk)

DOI: 10.1201/9781003599036

Typeset in Helvetica
by codeMantra

To KCH and all our
four-legged pals

Table of Contents

Special Thanks to…

The folks at Taylor & Francis Publishing

Jean Gillmore
Karenia Kaminski
Warren Drummond
James Fujii
Ian Gooding
Kathy Baur
Tom Sito
Mark Farquhar
Dan Boulos
Cynthia Ignacio
Teresa Powers
My Family

I couldn't have done it without all of you!

What Is Storyboard?

DOI: 10.1201/9781003599036-1

What is Storyboard?

What is storyboard? Think as if storyboards are a blueprint to what a film will look like. A storyboard shows lighting, emotions, action, atmosphere, geography.... Storyboards are a reflection of the script, drawn out and illustrated to visually describe what is in one's MIND'S EYE as one reads the script, a visual interpretation of the written word.

So, think as if you were reading a script or a book or story, and you're envisioning that story in your head as you're reading that story, by bringing it to life on the page. Think that every film is like a book. Every sequence is like a chapter! A good book or film will successfully spirit you away into a different world, you'll be glued to your seat, and time passes so quickly that the end couldn't be more gratifying. Storyboards have to be CLEAR, EXPRESSIVE, and have GOOD STAGING. Storyboards aid in the visual storytelling in the script.

My friend, James Fujii, said something amazing to me the other day... he said, **STORY IS LIFE**. In other words, storyboarding is bringing these characters to life. When the audience begins to see these characters think, from panel to panel, you've hooked your audience! Now making great story is for another book... but what I can tell you, there are tremendous resources on great scriptwriting, how to tell story in film, filmmaking and story, the history of filmmaking, etc. Robert McKee is a fantastic resource for story and scriptwriting, and Joseph Campbell is one of my favorite resources on mythology and the origins of mythology and storytelling. This book focuses primarily on storyboarding and the process of creating dynamic storyboards from a script.

Storyboarding helps to visually show that story, from "Once Upon a Time" to "The End" within a 1920 × 1080 px size, going from frame to frame to frame.

PANEL 1

WIDE ESTABLISHING SHOT

Detective Wallis enters a cave…

PANEL 2

MEDIUM SHOT

The man walks further into the cave.

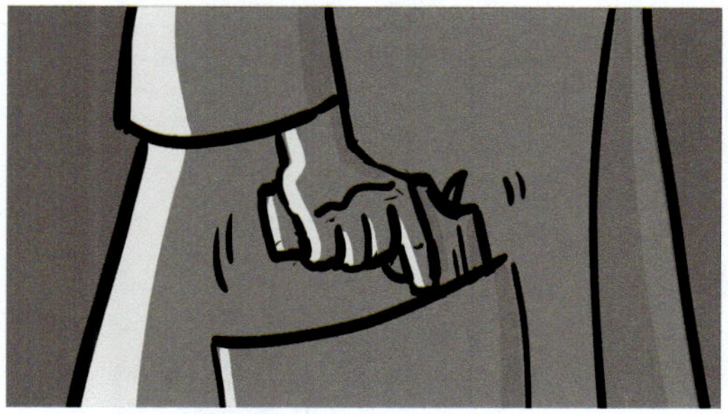

PANEL 3

CLOSE UP SHOT

The man pulls out a gun from his jacket pocket.

PANEL 4

MEDIUM SHOT, DUTCH ANGLE

The man aims his gun.

PANEL 5

MEDIUM SHOT/DUTCH ANGLE

But a shadow grows and he reacts…

PANEL 6

DOWN SHOT

… to the presence of a big bear!

PANEL 7

MEDIUM WIDE SHOT

The bear stares down at the detective…

PANEL 8

MEDIUM WIDE SHOT

The bear evilly grins as the man reacts.

2

Setup and Payoff

DOI: 10.1201/9781003599036-2

Setup and Payoff

How do I start making a great storyboard? The first thing you may want to do is start small, with just one page of a script, a simple conversation, or a greeting between two characters. This particular exchange should entail a SETUP and a PAYOFF.

What is SETUP?

A film or a book has a setup… one sets up the story, such as a "Once upon a time?" or "It all began with…" or "One day…,"

A film has several sequences, each of which has a setup.

First, we start with an idea, a story…

For example, here we have a story, called Mysterious Mysteries, the mysterious adventures of Jones and Bones, and like every story, we begin with a "Once Upon a Time…" which is the overall SETUP for your story.

Once upon a time...

Once upon a time, there were two best friends, Jones and Bones, who started a new business, a detective agency.

One day...

One day, they get a case**!** A gentleman hires the detective agency to solve a mystery of a large creature that is terrorizing his theme park.

And then...

And then in their investigations, they come across a huge flying creature that menaces them in a rollercoaster at the park. It is a harrowing experience!

But then...

But then Jones and Bones have a major disagreement, which threatens their friendship and their detective agency... and the case at hand!

And so...

And so, Jones and Bones resolve their issues, find the culprit and solve the case**!** (PAYOFF)

THE END

SETUP

The setup is just that... a setup! The story sets up a gag or a chain of events that will resolve itself within that sequence... and all those sequences follow the overall setup to resolve the entire film. The villain places the banana on the road for the protagonist to slip on... or a character enters the bar... or a character goes hunting for a giant beast...

PAYOFF

Payoff is when the character(s) wins or loses or learns and whatever the setup was has now been paid off with that win or loss. For example, the character slips on the banana and drops on their head... the character gets kicked out of the bar... the giant beast chases the hunter away...

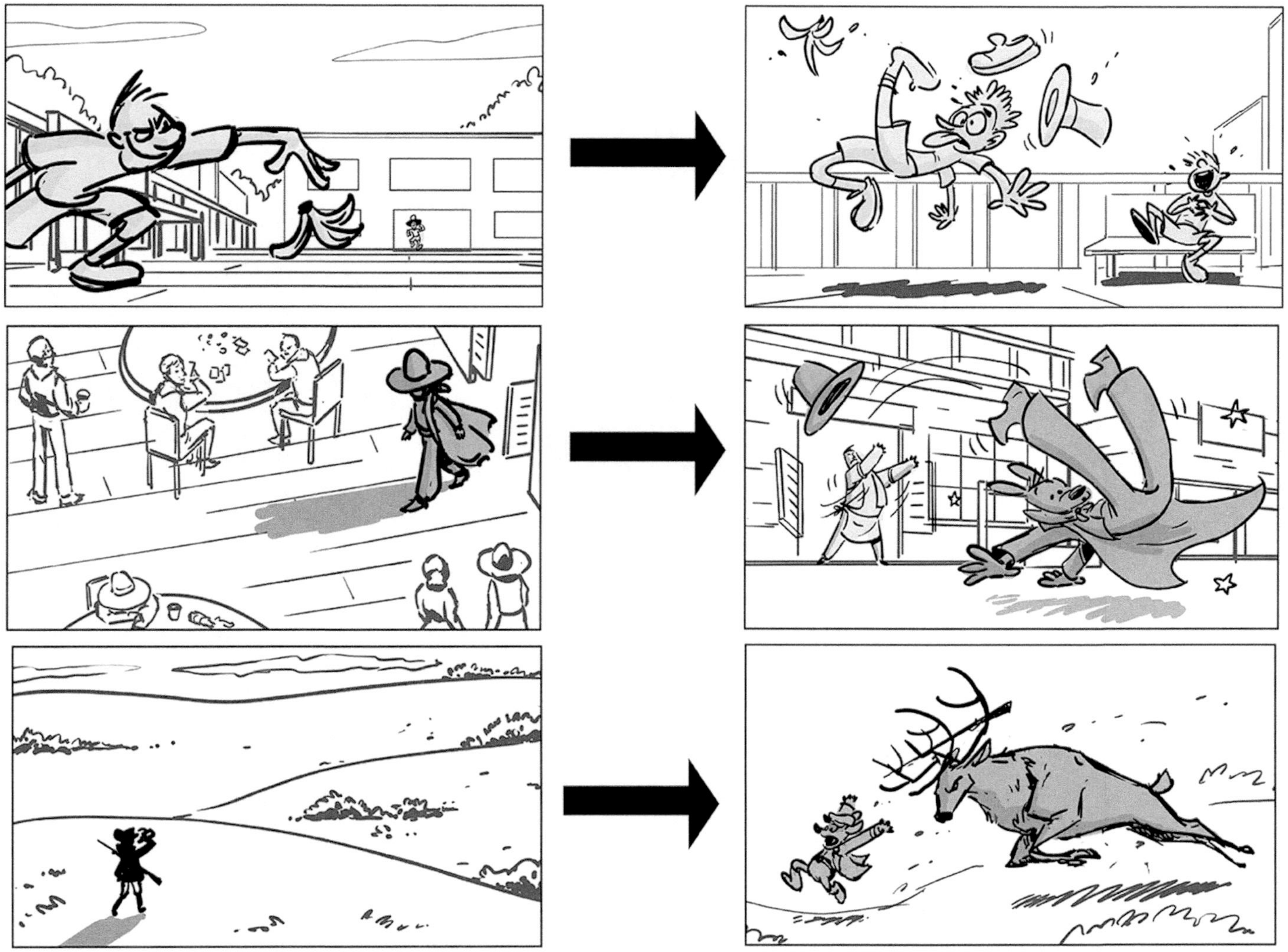

3

Clarity

DOI: 10.1201/9781003599036-3

Clarity

Communication is key when doing storyboards. Your storyboards have to be clear for your audience to understand or else your audience will be confused and ultimately lose interest in your story. Clarity in staging, character expressions, screen direction, tonals—everything! Remember the basic rules of composition:

The Rule of Thirds

The Rule of Thirds is a guideline where the focal point of that composition is placed at the cross points of one of the four cross sections of a 3×3 grid that is superimposed on the image.

The Golden Ratio

The Golden Ratio, or the approximate number 1.618, is often depicted in art in spirals within a rectangular frame. One usually uses this to visualize a divine proportion within the composition.

Depth: Foreground, Middle Ground, Background

Depth in a composition creates a three-dimensional illusion. One can create depth by creating foreground, middle ground, and background elements within the composition.

Depth can also be additionally created using three tonals within the composition: dark, medium, and light. Using these three groups of values can help determine dimensionality fairly easily. One can move within these three groups as one creates depth…

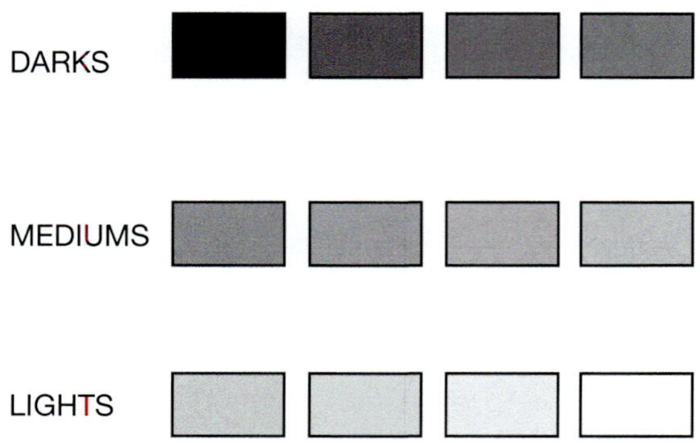

Balance

Balance in film refers to elements and characters arranged within a composition to achieve harmony and stability. One can achieve this by creating a symmetrical or asymmetrical composition and balance objects or characters within that composition.

FIGURE 15

Contrast

Contrast in film can be portrayed in tones, such as lights versus darks, bright versus dull, loud versus quiet, etc. and can be used to convey the emotion of the scene.

4

Color vs. Tonals

DOI: 10.1201/9781003599036-4

Color vs. Tonals

Most of the time, storyboards are drawn in black and white, emphasizing value, staging, composition, and character expressions… Color is often used in beat boards and advertising boards, to really sell an idea, concept, or story. In film storyboards, you will occasionally see a color panel here and there, to emphasize the drama of the scene or to distinguish characters. It is really your choice, but because of the sheer number of panels one has to draw, choose wisely if you wish to use color or tonals for your storyboard.

Once upon a time, a prince met a princess.

She pours a bottle of honey on him!

A bear chases him away.

The prince came a-wooing again.

He brought a cookie!

It is love at last…

So, she turns him into a frog…

And they live happily ever after!

Think that EVERY frame is a beautiful well-composed illustration, with the characters and background staged in the BEST, most clear composition, and BEST shows the action, emotion, mood, etc.

5

Blocking

DOI: 10.1201/9781003599036-5

Blocking

A simple approach…

The easiest and best way to make clear, easy-to-read storyboards is to do THUMBNAILS and BLOCK YOUR STORYBOARDS OUT.

So, what is BLOCKING?

Blocking uses SIMPLE SHAPES to create a balanced and cohesive composition within the storyboard frame. When blocking, one uses the CIRCLE, SQUARE, TRIANGLE, and LINE to place characters within a setting.

To practice, take a film you like… look at each shot and simplify each shot into these simple shapes…

Blocking with Squares

Blocking with Triangles

Blocking with Circles

Blocking with Lines

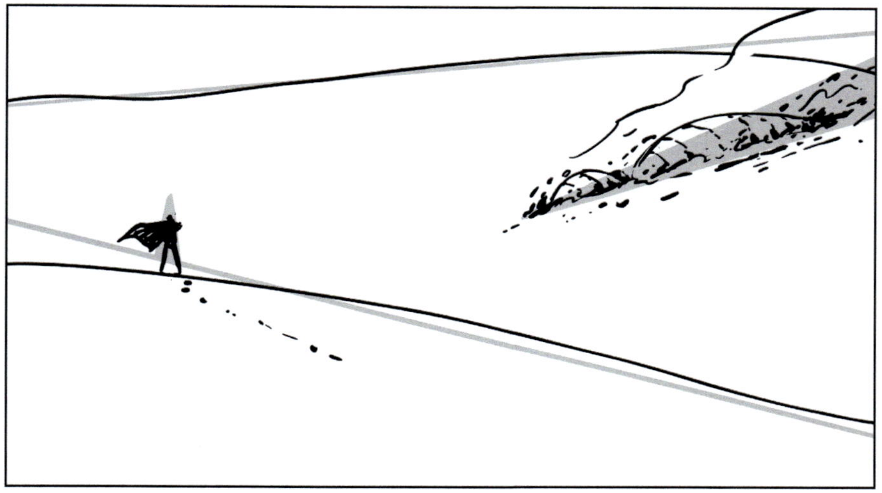

Putting It Together

In a composition, one puts all these basic elements—the circle, square, triangle, lines—together to create a balanced and beautiful composition within a shot!

6 Learning from the Classics

DOI: 10.1201/9781003599036-6

Learning from the Classics

We all love to watch films and shows! But there is nothing better to learn from than the classics, the black and white films… why? Because one is not worried about color and can sort out blocking more easily than if the film were in color.

Where to start? The AFI 100 is a great resource to start with your film education. This list contains a list of 100 films that epitomize great storytelling, great acting, and overall great filmmaking. This list is a great way to become a real student of film!

Blocking from watching the films you love really helps you learn about good composition and staging. And why?

1. You don't have to deal with color. You only need to analyze the shot in black and white.
2. The staging may be simpler, but if you're just a beginner, it will help to figure it using classic silent films.

It is important to be a student of film… It's fun to explore, go back in history and discover new stories, discover the context of when that film was made, how relationships were different from now, as well as overall storytelling. Studying and continually studying film will inform and improve your skills as a storyboard artist!

So, what are your favorite films, past and present?

Breaking Down the Classics

So, let's break down a few shots from the classics and block the shots. You can get creative with those simple shapes, but the principles are the same… triangulation, squares, circles, and lines. Again, you can choose any film that inspires you! First, watch it and enjoy it, then watch it with the sound off and begin breaking down the shots. You'll be amazed at how you'll soon understand and see how clear your staging becomes and how well designed these shots really are.

Silent films are my favorite to study. Whatever limitations silent film had back in the day certainly doesn't matter, as filmmakers still created beautifully composed and incredible stories. I broke these shots down from the classic silent film, Nosferatu, F.W. Murnau being one of the most elegant and sophisticated filmmakers.

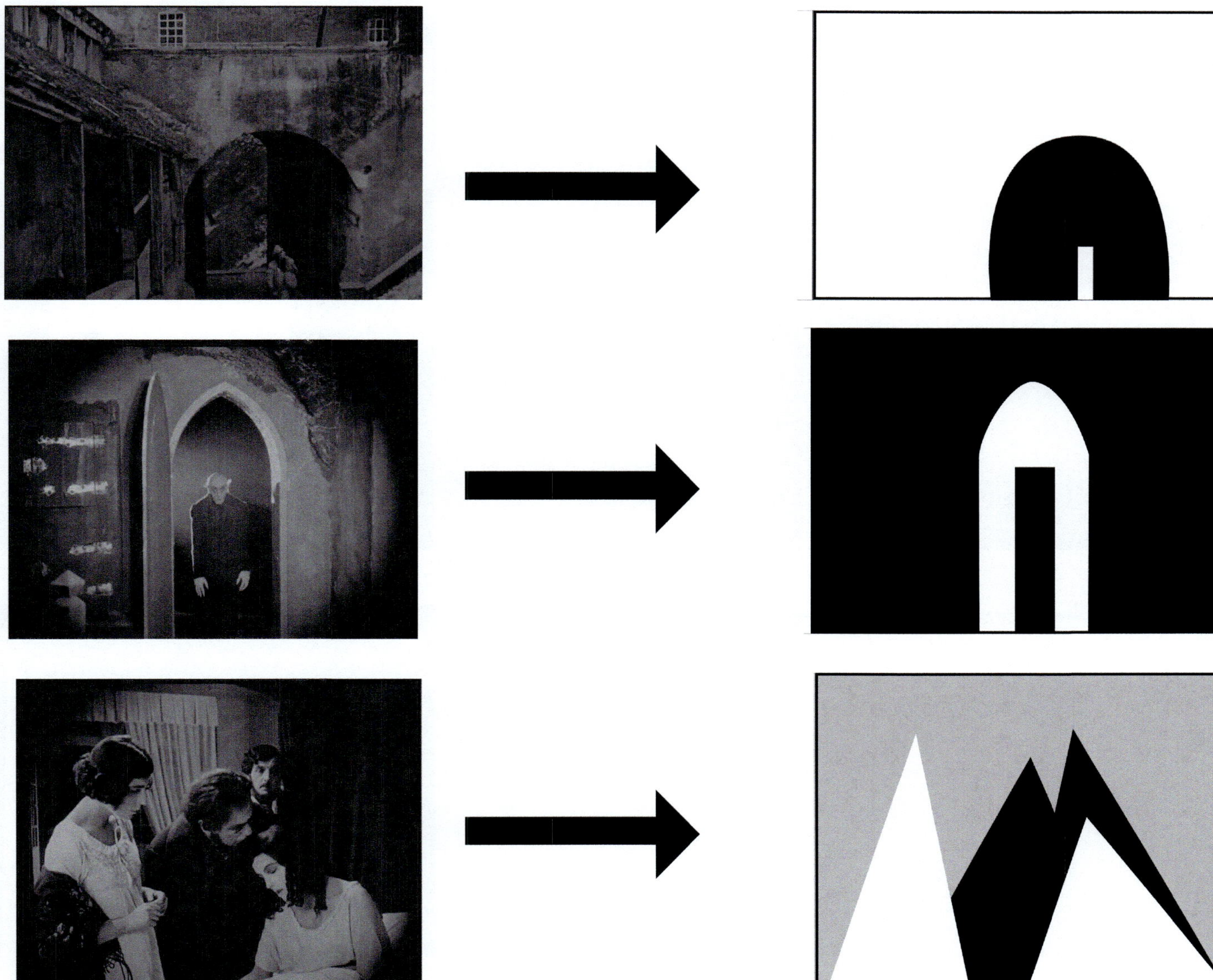

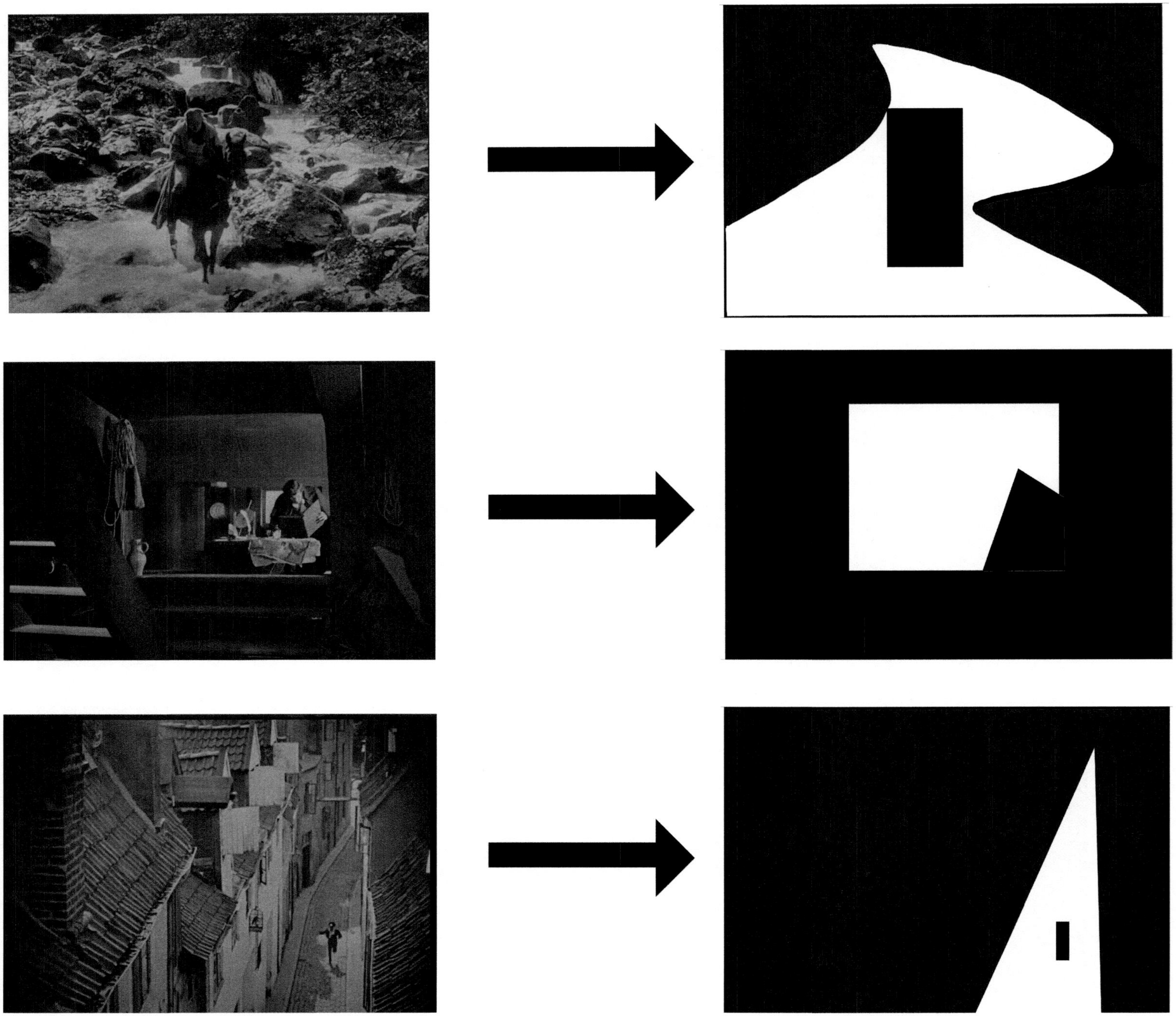

Thumbnails

DOI: 10.1201/9781003599036-7

Thumbnails

Another great way is to do thumbnails. This is a commonly used practice in storyboarding. One will read a script, sketch out rough stick figures, shapes, and staging in little boxes. Oftentimes, storyboard artists scratch out all the shots on a sketchbook, on the script itself, and problem solve or work out the kinks on any scrap paper. It can be messy but that's okay! It's one's own visual notes that one translates onto the actual storyboard. Oftentimes, it makes the storyboard process go a bit faster…

Check out this example, an excerpt from the play "Macbeth" by William Shakespeare, in which Lady Macbeth greets her husband, who returns to their room after having just killed the king, Duncan. Macbeth freaks out having done the deed, as Lady Macbeth tries desperately to calm his nerves to no avail. At the end of the scene, Macbeth has forgotten to leave the bloodied daggers with the king's attendants, to which his wife calls him weak and leaves to put the daggers back in place.

Enter Macbeth with bloody daggers.

LADY MACBETH My husband?

MACBETH I have done the deed. Didst thou not hear a noise?

LADY MACBETH I heard the owl scream and the crickets cry.

Did not you speak?

MACBETH When?

LADY MACBETH Now.

MACBETH As I descended?

LADY MACBETH Ay.

MACBETH Hark!—Who lies i' th' second chamber?

LADY MACBETH Donalbain.

MACBETH This is a sorry sight.

LADY MACBETH A foolish thought, to say a sorry sight.

MACBETH There's one did laugh in 's sleep, and one cried "Murder!"

That they did wake each other. I stood and heard them.

But they did say their prayers and addressed them

Again to sleep.

LADY MACBETH There are two lodged together.

MACBETH One cried "God bless us" and "Amen" the other,
As they had seen me with these hangman's hands,
List'ning their fear. I could not say "Amen"
When they did say "God bless us."
LADY MACBETH Consider it not so deeply.
MACBETH But wherefore could not I pronounce "Amen"?
I had most need of blessing, and "Amen"
Stuck in my throat.
LADY MACBETH These deeds must not be thought
After these ways; so, it will make us mad.
MACBETH Methought I heard a voice cry "Sleep no more!
Macbeth does murder sleep"—the innocent sleep,
Sleep that knits up the raveled sleave of care,
The death of each day's life, sore labor's bath,
Balm of hurt minds, great nature's second course,
Chief nourisher in life's feast.
LADY MACBETH What do you mean?
MACBETH Still it cried "Sleep no more!" to all the house.
"Glamis hath murdered sleep, and therefore
Cawdor shall sleep no more. Macbeth shall sleep no more."
LADY MACBETH Who was it that thus cried? Why, worthy thane,
You do unbend your noble strength to think
So brainsickly of things. Go get some water
And wash this filthy witness from your hand.—
Why did you bring these daggers from the place?
They must lie there. Go, carry them and smear
The sleepy grooms with blood.
MACBETH I'll go no more.
I am afraid to think what I have done.
Look on 't again I dare not.
LADY MACBETH Infirm of purpose!
Give me the daggers. The sleeping and the dead
Are but as pictures. 'Tis the eye of childhood
That fears a painted devil. If he do bleed,
I'll gild the faces of the grooms withal,
For it must seem their guilt.
She exits with the daggers.

Take those thumbnails, blow them up to approximately the same size as the panels, and tighten them up! Thumbnails are just a rough start, a quick way of working through staging, expressions, etc. The emphasis is to make sure your expressions and storyboards are clear, and your actions and staging are also clear. There are many software programs that also input your choice of notes automatically. In this case, this board was done and formatted in Storyboard Pro.

Scene 2 / Panel 1	Scene 2 / Panel 2	Scene 2 / Panel 3

Dialog LADY MACBETH My husband? 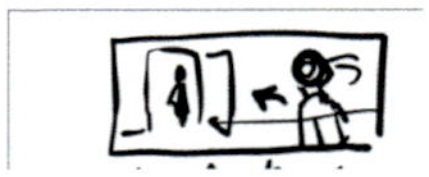	Dialog LADY MACBETH My husband?	Dialog MACBETH I have done the deed. 
Action Notes Enter Macbeth with bloody daggers.	Action Notes Enter Macbeth with bloody daggers.	

fig31

Scene	Panel
2	4

Dialog

MACBETH
Didst thou not hear the noise?

Scene	Panel
2	5

Dialog

LADY MACBETH
I heard the owl scream and the crickets cry.
Did not you speak?
MACBETH
When?
LADY MACBETH
Now.
MACBETH
As I descended?
LADY MACBETH
Ay.

Scene	Panel
2	6

Dialog

MACBETH
Hark! Who lies i' th' second chamber?
LADY MACBETH
Donalbain.

Scene	Panel
2	7

Dialog

MACBETH This is a sorry sight.

Scene	Panel
2	8

Scene	Panel
2	9

Dialog

LADY MACBETH

A foolish thought, to say a sorry sight.

Scene	Panel
2	10

Dialog

LADY MACBETH
A foolish thought, to say a sorry sight.

Scene	Panel
2	11

Dialog

MACBETH
There's one did laugh in 's sleep, and one cried
"Murder!"
That they did wake each other. I stood and heard
them.
But they did say their prayers and addressed them
Again to sleep.

Action Notes

Over The Shoulder Shot

Scene	Panel
2	12

Dialog

LADY MACBETH There are two lodged together.

Action Notes

Over The Shoulder Shot

Scene	Panel
2	13

Dialog

MACBETH

One cried "God bless us" and "Amen" the other,

As they had seen me with these hangman's hands,

List'ning their fear. I could not say "Amen"

When they did say "God bless us."

Scene	Panel
2	14

Dialog

LADY MACBETH Consider it not so deeply.

Scene	Panel
2	15

Dialog

MACBETH

But wherefore could not I pronounce "Amen"?

I had most need of blessing, and "Amen"

Stuck in my throat.

Action Notes

Reverse Shot

Scene	Panel
2	16

Dialog

LADY MACBETH These deeds must not be thought
After these ways; so, it will make us mad.

Scene	Panel
3	1

Dialog

MACBETH Methought I heard a voice cry "Sleep no more!
Macbeth does murder sleep"—the innocent sleep,
Sleep that knits up the raveled sleave of care,
The death of each day's life, sore labor's bath,
Balm of hurt minds, great nature's second course,
Chief nourisher in life's feast.
LADY MACBETH What do you mean?
MACBETH Still it cried "Sleep no more!" to all the house.
"Glamis hath murdered sleep, and therefore
Cawdor shall sleep no more. Macbeth shall sleep no more."

Scene	Panel
4	1

Dialog

LADY MACBETH
Who was it that thus cried? Why, worthy thane,
You do unbend your noble strength to think
So brainsickly of things. Go get some water

Scene	Panel
4	2

Dialog

And wash this filthy witness from your hand.—
Why did you bring these daggers from the place?
They must lie there. Go, carry them and smear
The sleepy grooms with blood.

Scene	Panel
4	3

Dialog

MACBETH I'll go no more.
I am afraid to think what I have done.

Scene	Panel
4	4

Dialog

MACBETH Look on 't again I dare not.

Scene	Panel
4	5

Dialog

LADY MACBETH   Infirm of purpose!
Give me the daggers. The sleeping and the dead
Are but as pictures. 'Tis the eye of childhood
That fears a painted devil. If he do bleed,

Action Notes

Wide Shot.

Scene	Panel
4	6

Dialog

LADY MACBETH If he do bleed,
I'll gild the faces of the grooms withal,
For it must seem their guilt.

Action Notes

She exits with the daggers.

Scene	Panel
4	7

Action Notes

Close Up on Macbeth.

8

Storyboards vs. Comic Books

DOI: 10.1201/9781003599036-8

Storyboards vs. Comic Books

Storyboards are, of course, restricted to one filmic format, which is typically a 1920×1080 format. Comics are confined to a vertical moving web comic format or to a comic book page.

In comics, one can take liberties with staging, and the image box can take different shapes or no shape at all, all within the comic book page.

For example, this is a comic book page of two men in an empty landscape and see an approaching figure, who brings mayhem to the scene.

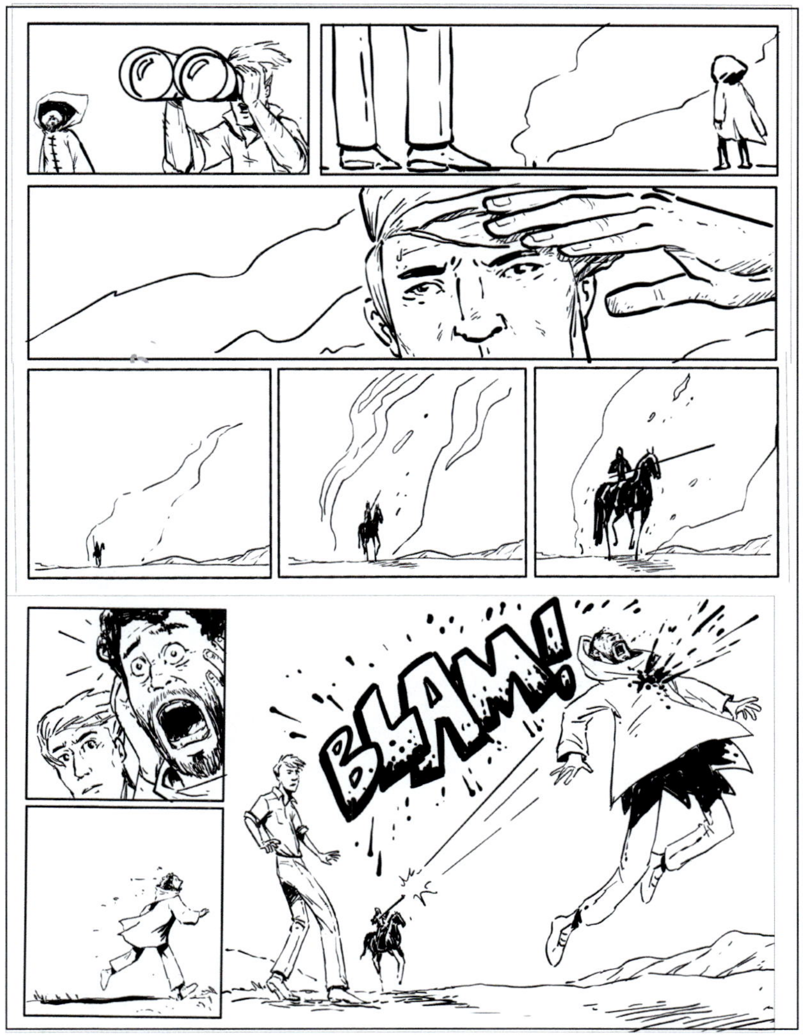

One can tell the SAME story in storyboards, animation, or live action. In storyboards, one is confined to the 1920×1080 pixels or 4×3 inches dimensions, shots are spelled out in a manner in which one sees the story through one's mind's eye...

Typical storyboard dimensions are 4″×3″, so if you print out your boards for a "shot list," which is typically used by live action, you can stack three boards on an 8.5″×11″ paper. In the below example, I have stacked four panels side by side on a landscape page, with scene and panel labels clearly indicated above each panel. It is imperative to be neat and orderly when you present your storyboards as this "film blueprint" is shared with much of the crew, so professionalism is key. Your drawings need to be clean and clear, as does your presentation.

It is a good idea to build your shot list as you go... Working with a director who knows what shot they want for each scene is very helpful!

9

Beat Boards

DOI: 10.1201/9781003599036-9

Beat Boards

What are beat boards? Beat boards are a broad visual swath of your story, exhibiting the key points of your story. You're visually telling your audience, in very broad terms, box by box, what happens to your characters in your story from beginning to end. Beat boards read like a children's picture book, with each illustration describing a line or paragraph of the story.

When doing beat boards, you can create prompts that will help illustrate what is happening in your story:

ONCE UPON A TIME… Mr. Bones lived in a house on a hill far away from Mr. Jones.

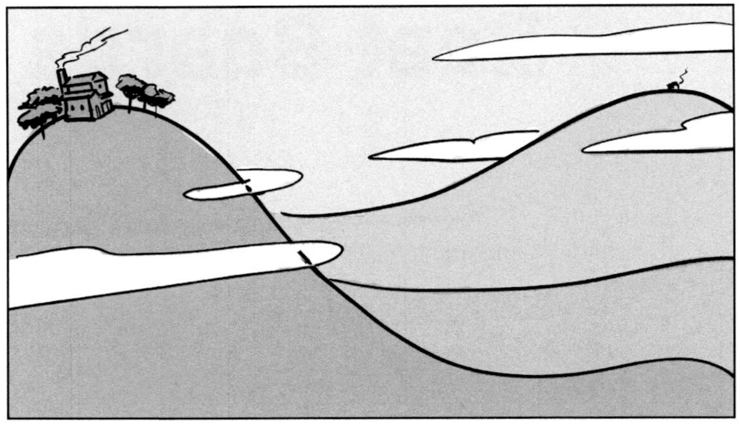

ONE DAY, Mr. Bones receives a letter, asking him to come to Mr. Jones's house for tea.

BUT it's raining! He gathers his coat and umbrella and leaves.

So he goes through several obstacles, like a large puddle in his path. He uses his large umbrella to cross the large puddle.

MEANWHILE his pal, Mr. Jones, worries as he makes the tea. He starts a fire to warm the house and thinks where Mr. Bones has possibly gone, and studies a map.

SUDDENLY Mr. Bones gets stuck in the mud. Miraculously Mr. Jones shows up to save Mr. Bones with a rope.

FINALLY, Mr. Jones and Mr. Bones make their way to Mr. Jones's house and recover and enjoy their tea by the fire.

10

Live Action vs. Animation

DOI: 10.1201/9781003599036-10

Live Action vs. Animation

Storyboards have certainly come a long way since the early days of Hitchcock and Kurosawa, but the approach has always been the same… great illustrations acting as guidelines for the director, actors, cinematographer, and lighting. The format was pretty loose in the early days of film, and when analog television came around, TV storyboard formats became typically more square in shape, to accommodate the square size for the analog television camera. Because analog televisions did not match the big screen, story artists drew boards in these squares and wrestled with creating great compositions within this square space. When flat screen televisions came around, video formats as well as storyboard formats evolved to match the big screen: 1920 × 1080.

LIVE ACTION STORYBOARDS emphasize composition, camera moves, action, staging, and the emotion of the scene. These boards are blueprints for many members of the crew: cinematographer, lighting, director, actors, stunts, etc. Live action boards are beautiful illustrations, great compositions in black and white, realistic in style. Live actions boards can be done in animatics, which can be especially useful for complex camera moves, but most boards are used in a binder called the "shot list," which is a document used by the director and other crew members to determine what shots will be used for the scene.

Should you use arrows?

In live action, arrows are frequently used to indicate direction of the character, object (like cars or spaceships, etc.) or camera moves. Arrows are used to help anyone in the crew determine what needs to be done in that particular shot.

In animation, arrows are less frequently used, as characters are drawn in a key frame animation to indicate action and movement through a scene, in an animatic. Animation storyboards are nowadays done as key frame animation in animatics, which can include layout, sound and music, and timing. It is important to learn to animate and understand animation fundamentals, gain skills in perspective and layout, as well as understand filmmaking rules and timing in order to help you be an effective story artist.

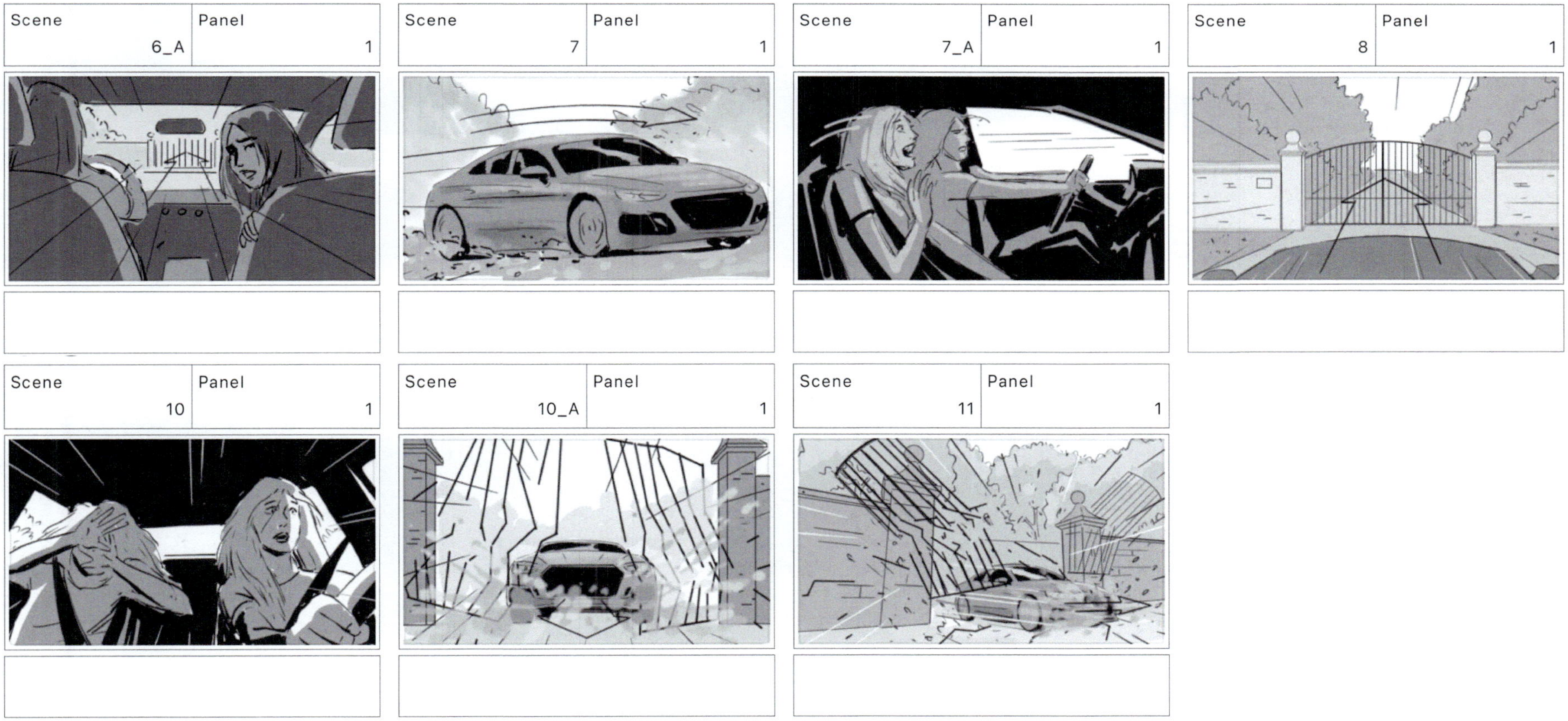

ANIMATION STORYBOARDS these days have become storyboard animatics, emphasizing key frame animation, clear layout, action, staging, and character expressiveness. These types of animatics are very often used in television. Drawing the characters on model as characters express emotions and move through each scene, drawing the accurate layout and staging, making boards clear for the production crew to use.

Using this example of Lady Macbeth entering a scene, walking in her sleep and washing her hands in a harried and frenetic motion, talking in her sleep as her doctor and nurse look on.

Scene 8	Panel 1	GENTLEWOMAN Neithe

Dialog
GENTLEWOMAN Neither to you nor anyone, having no witness to confirm my speech.

Action Notes
MEDIUM SHOT

Scene 8	Panel 2	Lo you, here she comes.

Dialog
Lo you, here she comes. This is her very guise and, upon my life, fast asleep. Observe her; stand close.

Action Notes
MEDIUM SHOT

Scene 8	Panel 3	

Action Notes
MEDIUM SHOT
Enter Lady ⌜Macbeth⌝ with a taper.

Scene 8	Panel 4	

Action Notes
MEDIUM SHOT
Enter Lady ⌜Macbeth⌝ with a taper.

Scene 8	Panel 5	DOCTOR How came s

Dialog
DOCTOR How came she by that light?

Action Notes
OVER THE SHOULDER SHOT

Scene 8	Panel 6	GENTLEWOMAN Why, it

Dialog
GENTLEWOMAN Why, it stood by her. She has light by her continually. 'Tis her command.

Action Notes
OVER THE SHOULDER SHOT

Scene 8	Panel 7	GENTLEWOMAN Why, it

Dialog
GENTLEWOMAN Why, it stood by her. She has light by her continually. 'Tis her command.

Action Notes
OVER THE SHOULDER SHOT PAN RIGHT.
Lady Macbeth kneels.

Scene 8	Panel 8	

Action Notes
LOW SHOT

Scene 8	Panel 9	

Action Notes
LOW SHOT

Scene 8	Panel 10	

Action Notes
LOW SHOT ZOOM IN TO CLOSE UP

11

Perspective

DOI: 10.1201/9781003599036-11

Perspective

It is important to know the basics of perspective, as it pertains to drawing the proper layouts within your panels... Drawing the proper perspective for your shots can make your storyboards more dynamic as well as accurate! Perspective is very useful and imperative for creating depth and space in your visual storytelling. It is a great idea to map out where your character(s) is stationed and how your character(s) moves along in a landscape from A to Z in your story.

There are three basic perspectives to understand: one-, two-, and three-point perspectives. Let's take a look at each...

One-Point Perspective

In a one-point perspective, there is only ONE vanishing point on the horizon line. Everything, such as buildings, parked cars, and mailboxes, can all point to that one point on the horizon. Think as if you were looking straight down a hallway or down a street, gazing toward the horizon, with the lines and forms a creating the illusion of space, depth, and size variation.

The horizon line matches the viewer's eyeline. The vanishing point can be anywhere on that horizon line within the cone of vision.

Here's more examples of one perspectives…

For Over the Shoulder POV shots, be aware of where you place your camera… A common mistake is, for example, when you draw a character walking down a hallway… take note of where you place your horizon line. Is the horizon line high up on the shot or low?

Here's more examples of one perspectives…

For Over the Shoulder POV shots, be aware of where you place your camera… A common mistake is, for example, when you draw a character walking down a hallway… take note of where you place your horizon line. Is the horizon line high up on the shot or low?

If you draw this perspective, your camera is low to the ground, like this…

TWO-POINT PERSPECTIVES have TWO vanishing points on the horizon line, a left and right vanishing point. Typically, these two vanishing points sit far to the left and the right of the cone of vision and will not be located within your shots… In a two-point perspective, you will see a corner of two walls, whether it is an exterior or interior location.

Things like buildings and walls will run to either the left or right vanishing points. In this example, the windows, cabinets, bed, boxes, and pictures on the wall all point to both vanishing points.

Two-point perspectives are very useful and frequently used for doing exteriors and interiors.

THREE-POINT PERSPECTIVE is useful if your character(s) is a bird, airplane, or superhero looking DOWN upon a landscape

OR

if your character(s) is tiny like an insect, mouse, child, craning one's neck up to look high up at a very large high object.

Three-point perspectives use three vanishing points, on an X, Y, and Z axes. When one is looking down in the shot, the Z axis is very far down from the shot, whereas when one is looking up in the shot, the Z axis is very far high up from the shot.

Knowing where your character goes, you can use perspective to help you with your storyboards.

Example: map out where the characters go from A to Z in the scene. For example, one character, Vasquez, is on the loft, spots another character, Jillian, who leaps across the table, crashes through the window to land on a passing bus, which turns left down a street.

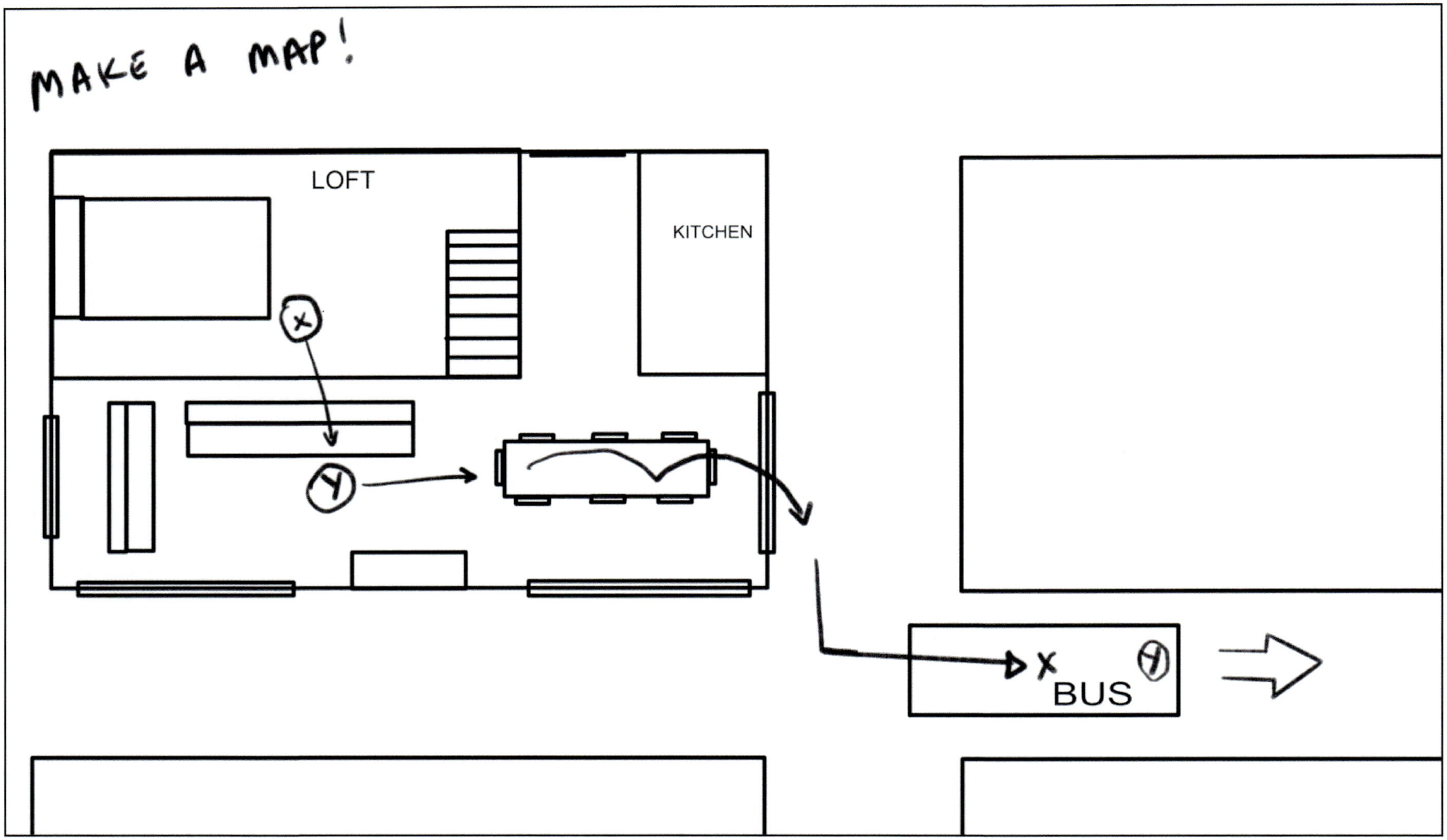

Using this map, we can now stage our storyboard, knowing exactly where our characters, Vasquez and Jillian, are going to go, starting from the loft, out the window, and onto an ongoing bus. Note the different opportunities to change your perspectives in this action sequence.

Scene	Panel
7	1

Action Notes

TWO POINT PERSPECTIVE

X spots Y at the dining table.

Scene	Panel
8	1

Action Notes

TWO POINT PERSPECTIVE DOWN SHOT

X leaps over the ledge towards Y, on the first floor of the apartment.

Scene	Panel
9	1

Action Notes

Y places the weapon in their jacket.

Scene	Panel
10	1

Action Notes

LOW SHOT TWO POINT PERSPECTIVE

X jumps down and lands on the first floor as Y jumps up on the table and runs screen left towards the large window.

Scene	Panel
10	2

Action Notes

LOW SHOT TWO POINT PERSPECTIVE

Scene	Panel
10	3

Action Notes

LOW SHOT TWO POINT PERSPECTIVE

Scene	Panel
11	1

Action Notes

ONE POINT PERSPECTIVE

Y crashes through the large window. X follows.

Scene	Panel
12	1

Action Notes

UP SHOT TWO POINT PERSPECTIVE

X notes Y jump out of the building.

Scene 13 | Panel 1

Action Notes

DOWN SHOT THREE POINT PERSPECTIVE

X watches Y land on an ongoing bus.

Scene 14 | Panel 1

Action Notes

ONE POINT PERSPECTIVE

X looks on.

Scene 14 | Panel 2

Action Notes

ONE POINT PERSPECTIVE

X runs back to the end of the room.

Scene 14 | Panel 3

Action Notes

ONE POINT PERSPECTIVE

X takes a running start.

Scene 14 | Panel 4

Action Notes

ONE POINT PERSPECTIVE

X runs towards the open window.

Scene 15 | Panel 1

Action Notes

UP SHOT TWO POINT PERSPECTIVE

X jumps out the window in pursuit of Y.

Scene 16 | Panel 1

Action Notes

TRACKING SHOT

X falls.

Scene 17 | Panel 1

Action Notes

LOW SHOT TWO POINT PERSPECTIVE

X lands on the road, as the RV drives away.

Scene	Panel
17	2

Action Notes
LOW SHOT TWO POINT PERSPECTIVE

X runs after the RV, as it turns a corner.

Scene	Panel
18	1

Action Notes
TRACKING SHOT

X runs after the RV.

Scene	Panel
19	1

Action Notes
DOWN SHOT

X reaches for the ladder on the back of the RV.

Scene	Panel
19	2

Action Notes
DOWN SHOT

X climbs up the ladder on the RV.

Scene	Panel
20	1

Action Notes
LOW SHOT ONE POINT PERSPECTIVE

X reaches the top of the RV.

Scene	Panel
20	2

Action Notes
LOW SHOT ONE POINT PERSPECTIVE

Y reacts as X reaches the top of the RV.

Scene	Panel
21	1

Action Notes
ONE POINT PERSPECTIVE

X points to Y.

Scene	Panel
22	1

Action Notes
WIDE SHOT THREE POINT PERSPECTIVE

X demands Y return the knife.

12

Staging

DOI: 10.1201/9781003599036-12

Staging

Before we get into what to do about SHOTS, we need to understand the importance of staging. Staging is where you place your characters on the stage/camera frame and direct where they go from scene to scene, and where this character is in relation to objects/scenery/other characters.

So, where are your characters in the scene, and where are they going?

Screen Left

If your character is "screen left," your character is literally on the LEFT of the frame…

OR the character is moving toward the LEFT side of the screen.

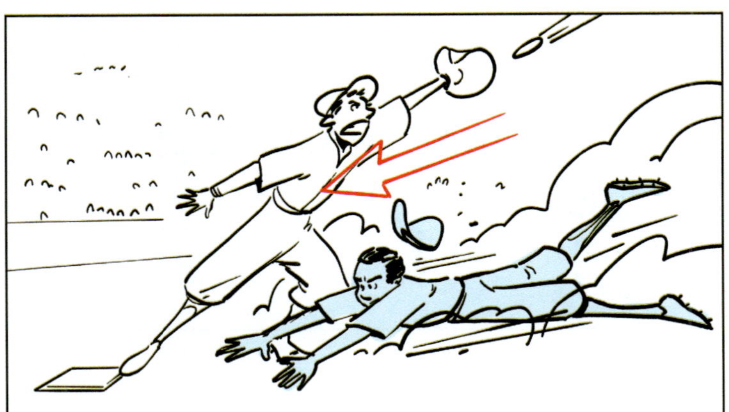

Screen Right

And if your character is "screen right," your character is literally on the RIGHT of the frame…

OR the character is moving toward the RIGHT side of the screen.

If your character on, for example, the LEFT side switches sides with the character on the RIGHT, then that character is now screen LEFT, and every subsequent shot must show that character on the LEFT side of the screen.

Mr. Pink is on the left! En guard!

Huzzah! Mr. Pink SWITCHES to the right!!

Take that! Mr. Pink is now on the right!

Ouch!

All this refers to **CROSSING THE 180.** When you storyboard, say a pitcher and a hitter in a baseball game, the camera will remain on the right side of the pitcher and in your storyboard, the pitcher will always remain on the LEFT side of your panels. The pitcher cannot be staged on the RIGHT SIDE, which is the NO GO ZONE. If you cross this imaginary line, you can create a disorienting effect on the viewer, which can cause problems for your story!

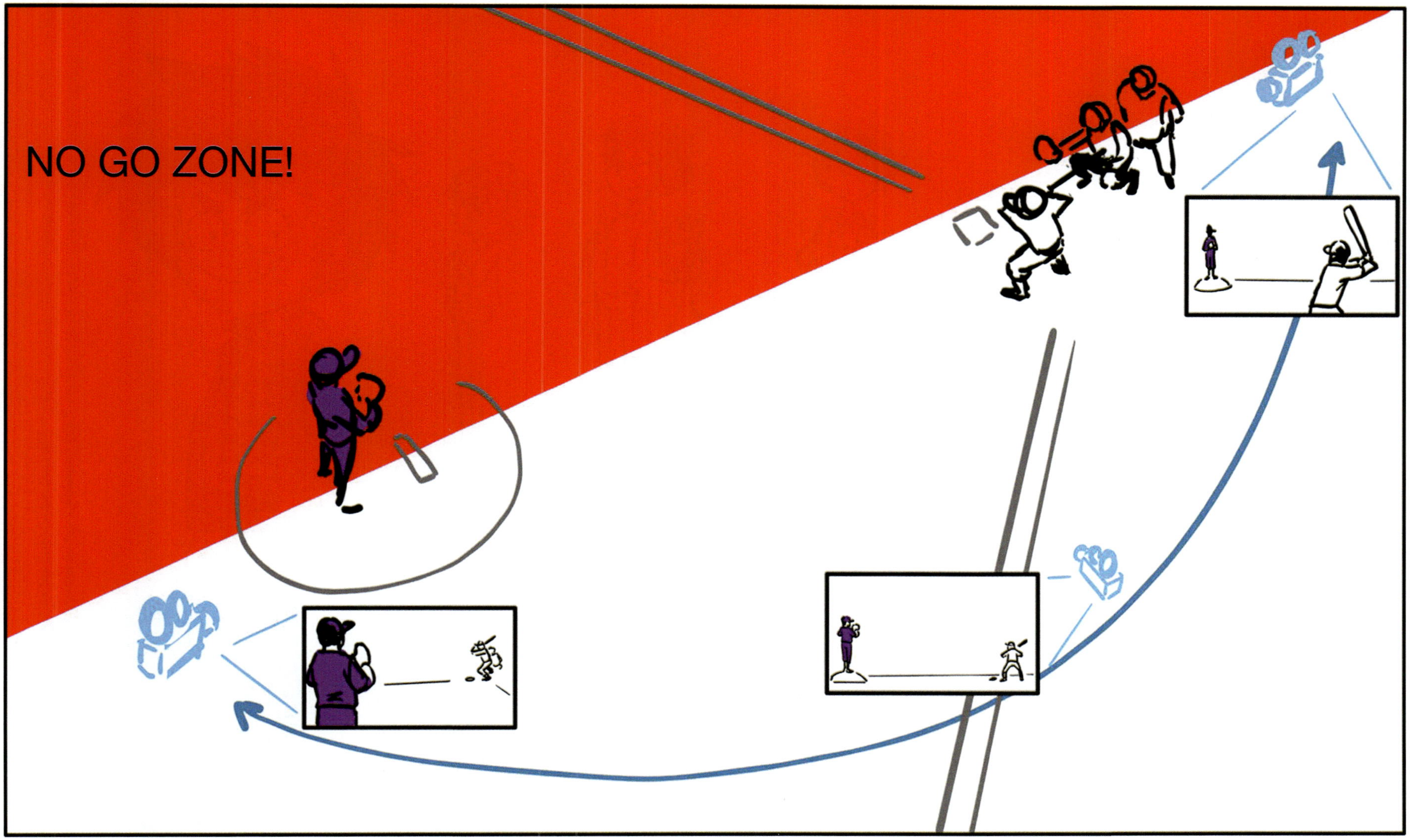

13

Drawing Expressions in Storyboards

DOI: 10.1201/9781003599036-13

Drawing Expressions on Characters and in Storyboards

It is imperative to draw clear and expressive characters in animation. Push your poses as much as you can and stage the character in a clear and most optimal angle of your shot that is relevant to your story. Expressions can be shown in a multitude of ways… as long it is clear.

One can stage CONTEMPLATIVE like this…

Or happiness…

Or sadness…

Or fear and suspense…

14 The Shots

DOI: 10.1201/9781003599036-14

The Shots

Like a book, films are a story told in sequences, i.e., chapters. Within these sequences are scenes that play out and take the character or characters from A to B, until the very end of the story.

Creating these shots is a lot like telling the story within the spirit of that story. For example, is your story a comedy? Then perhaps, you may have a lot of wide and medium wide shots to show the physicality and comedy of your characters with the scenes. Or is your story a funky, fast-paced tongue in cheek type of story? Then you may want to research interesting and quirky shots and a multitude of variations of shots.

Staging your shots is critical in visual storytelling. It is important to ask yourself WHY you would choose a particular shot and if it is optimally reflecting what is going on in one's mind's eye within the story. Conscientious storyboarding can dictate a sophistication to you telling your visual story.

Stage your characters… where do they stand and why they stand in relation to each other and which direction they travel within the scene. The following are the various shots utilized on film.

Wide Shots are often establishing shots, showing an entire landscape or setting within one shot. Wide shots are strong in perspective and can be shown at any angle…

Wide shots portray settings, establish place, a world… Wide shots are typically used as establishing shots to open a sequence or story.

Medium Closeups are also frequently used and can depict a more emotional communication or emotional view of the character.

Extreme Closeups focus on a key point or object in a scene, for example, a lost book, an eye, a hand touching a precious object, etc.

Closeup Shots are all about getting inside the character's head, looking into the actor's eyes, emotions... closeups read an actor's thoughts as they move through a scene.

A Cowboy Shot shows a character in the shot from the knees up, almost as if the character is about to draw their guns from their holsters.

Down Shots can show characters in a weak state, they can depict the characters as powerless, small. On a down shot, a three-point perspective is most useful to illustrate building structures and perspectives.

Dutch Angle Shots create a feeling of chaos, an almost upside-down world.

Medium Shots are the most often used shots… Medium shots can have two or more characters and can depict a verbal exchange or any other form of communication between characters.

OTS, or Over The Shoulder Shots, show a geographical relationship between two or more characters, with the camera view pointing over the shoulder of a character and toward the setting and the other characters. OTS shots are typically a POV shot, showing what that character is looking at.

Up Shots can show characters in a powerful position, as one can show the character in a larger-than-life point of view. Three-point perspective is also useful here as well.

A **Jump Cut** is a deliberate cut in the sequential flow of a film or storyboard, oftentimes to show a jump in time. For example, as shown below, a character can "jump" forward in time as the character jumps forward in age and in place. Jump cuts can be jarring but that is the intent!

Camera Moves

Camera moves are especially important and a great tool to show action, geography between characters, and the action… There are just the basics:

Camera moves can be dynamic, tell actions, draw attention to something.

A **CAMERA PAN** is a camera move that travels to the LEFT or to the RIGHT… A camera move can also PAN UP or PAN DOWN or at any angle. This camera move can be used to reveal or to track an object or character across a landscape or scene.

Pan Down

In this type of shot, the camera is panning DOWN a scene or a background.

This can also be considered a Dolly Shot which is a shot that follows the character(s) as they move through a scene. Typically, the camera is placed on a moveable track known as a dolly and shoots a character as they track through the shot. Dolly shots track the actions of characters through scenes.

You can do an elaborate PAN UP, do a ZOOM IN, TRACK your character in a DOLLY shot as your character moves through the scene. Make sure you are clear on your camera moves.

Camera moves are representative of your mind's eye! As you, the audience, are "reading" a story or script, you're "watching" this character move through the scene. Have fun doing camera moves; it can make your storyboard truly reflect your story in an effective way!

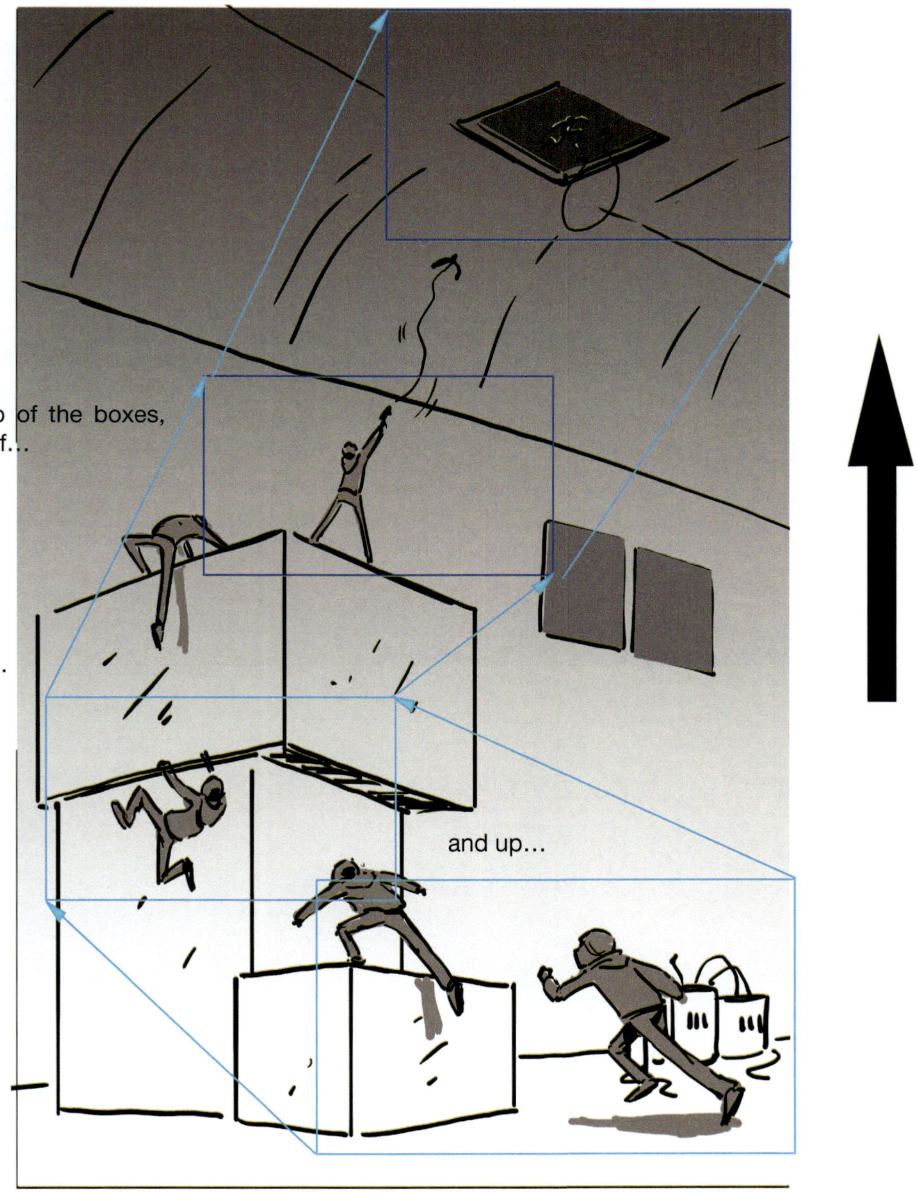

In this scene, the camera tracks the character as they leap up some boxes…

and up…

until at last, they reach the top of the boxes, shoot an anchor through the roof…

which allows them to leap through the roof and into freedom.

A **ZOOM IN** camera move can do things like emphasize the character's emotions or actions. A ZOOM IN puts emphasis on the scene.

A **ZOOM OUT** camera move can be used to reveal something or someone otherwise unseen. It can go from a closeup shot to an even wider shot.

Zoom In

Zoom Out

A **RACK FOCUS** is also often used and similar, in that the camera move places emphasis on where you want the audience to look. The RACK FOCUS shifts focus from one subject to another and shifts attention from one to the next.

Panel 1

Panel 2

A **DOLLY SHOT** follows a character(s) as they pass through a background… In a dolly shot, the background moves, and the camera is tracking alongside the character.

shot 1

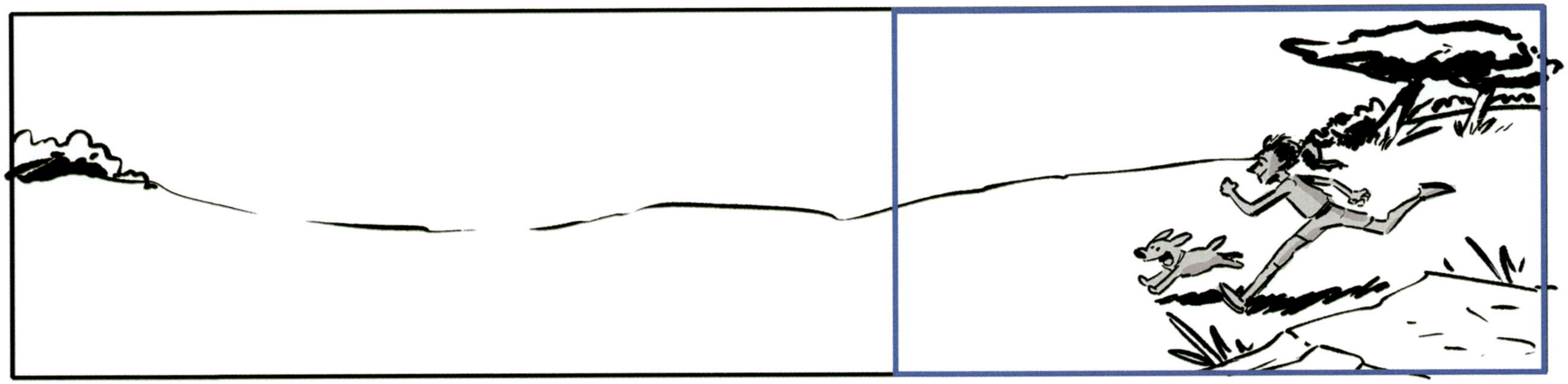

shot 2

shot 3

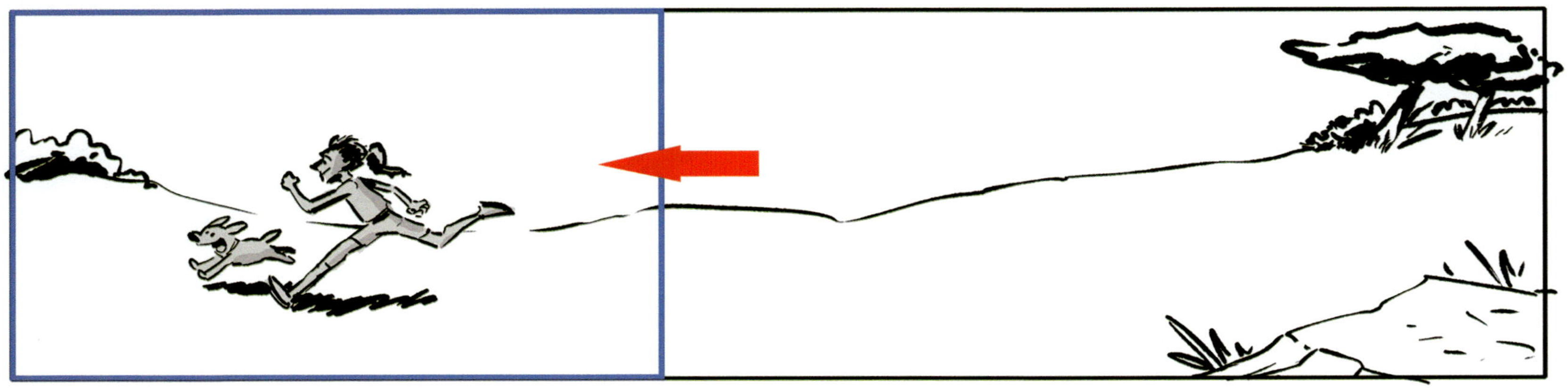

15

Putting It All Together

DOI: 10.1201/9781003599036-15

Putting It All Together

Be sure to vary your shots!

Shots tell a visual story whether it is a comedy, drama, action, documentary, advertising, etc. Ask yourself first," Is this the BEST shot that BEST explains what is going on in the scene? "Then ask yourself, "Is it clear?"

Let's try and make a storyboard… Take a script, just a page and start with thumbnails… in this example, we take a scene from Shakespeare's Macbeth, in which Macbeth and his friend, Banquo, meet the three Witches, who foretell ominous fortunes to both men. Banquo receives the message that his children will become kings, while Macbeth receives the omen that he shall be king. While Macbeth begs to hear more, the Witches disappear. Banquo believes this all to be a weird dream, while Macbeth is entranced by this fortune, thus beginning the turn of murderous events that encompass this play.

Enter Macbeth and Banquo.

MACBETH

So foul and fair a day I have not seen.

BANQUO

How far is 't called to 'Forres?'—What are these,

So withered, and so wild in their attire,

That look not like th' inhabitants o' th' Earth

And yet are on 't?—Live you? Or are you aught

That man may question? You seem to understand me

By each at once her choppy finger laying

Upon her skinny lips. You should be women,

And yet your beards forbid me to interpret

That you are so.

MACBETH vSpeak if you can. What are you?

FIRST WITCH

All hail, Macbeth! Hail to thee, Thane of Glamis!

SECOND WITCH

All hail, Macbeth! Hail to thee, Thane of Cawdor!

THIRD WITCH

All hail, Macbeth, that shalt be king hereafter!

BANQUO

Good sir, why do you start and seem to fear
Things that do sound so fair?—I' th' name of truth,
Are you fantastical, or that indeed
Which outwardly you show? My noble partner
You greet with present grace and great prediction
Of noble having and of royal hope,
That he seems rapt withal. To me you speak not.
If you can look into the seeds of time
And say which grain will grow and which will not,
Speak, then, to me, who neither beg nor fear
Your favors nor your hate.

FIRST WITCH Hail!

SECOND WITCH Hail!

THIRD WITCH Hail!

FIRST WITCH

Lesser than Macbeth and greater.

SECOND WITCH

Not so happy, yet much happier.

THIRD WITCH

Thou shalt get kings, though thou be none.
So all hail, Macbeth and Banquo!

FIRST WITCH

Banquo and Macbeth, all hail!

MACBETH

Stay, you imperfect speakers. Tell me more.
By Sinel's death I know I am Thane of Glamis.
But how of Cawdor? The Thane of Cawdor lives
A prosperous gentleman, and to be king
Stands not within the prospect of belief,
No more than to be Cawdor. Say from whence
You owe this strange intelligence or why
Upon this blasted heath you stop our way
With such prophetic greeting. Speak, I charge you.

Witches vanish.

BANQUO

The earth hath bubbles, as the water has,
And these are of them. Whither are they vanished?

MACBETH

Into the air, and what seemed corporal melted,
As breath into the wind. Would they had stayed!

BANQUO

Were such things here as we do speak about?
Or have we eaten on the insane root
That takes the reason prisoner?

MACBETH

Your children shall be kings.

BANQUO You shall be king.

From these thumbnails, we can flesh out and tighten up storyboards…

Scene	Duration	Panel	Duration
1	01:00	1	01:00

Dialog

MACBETH
So foul and fair a day I have not seen.

Action Notes

Super Wide Shot
Banquo and Macbeth walk up a hill.

Scene	Duration	Panel	Duration
2	03:00	1	01:00

Dialog

BANQUO
How far is 't called to ⌜Forres?⌝—

Action Notes

Master Shot/ Wide Shot
Banquo and Macbeth look around, as they walk.

Scene	Duration	Panel	Duration
2	03:00	2	01:00

Dialog

BANQUO
How far is 't called to ⌜Forres?⌝—

Action Notes

They react.

Scene	Duration	Panel	Duration
2	03:00	3	01:00

Dialog

BANQUO
How far is 't called to ⌜Forres?⌝—

Action Notes

Banquo and Macbeth draw their swords.

Scene	Duration	Panel	Duration
3	05:00	1	01:00

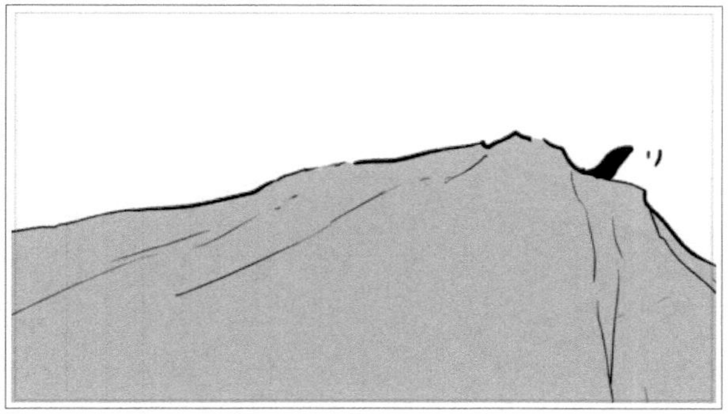

Action Notes

Wide Up Shot/ POV Shot
On the top of the hill, a creature rises up and reveals themselves to be the THREE WITCHES.

Scene	Duration	Panel	Duration
3	05:00	2	01:00

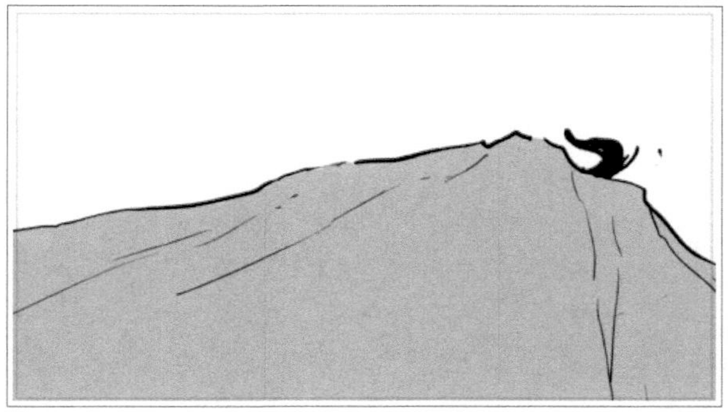

Scene	Duration	Panel	Duration
3	05:00	3	01:00

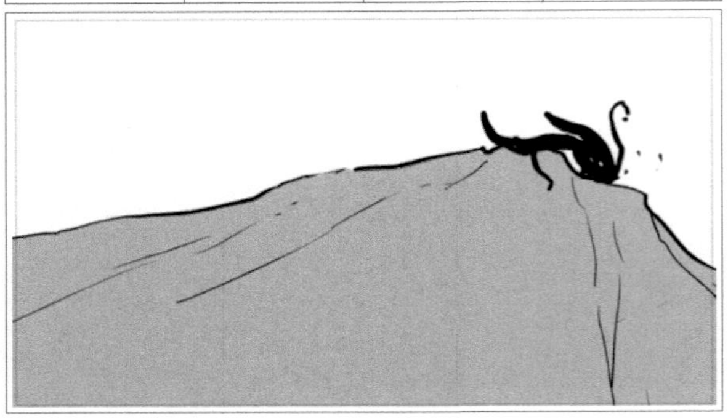

Scene	Duration	Panel	Duration
3	05:00	4	01:00

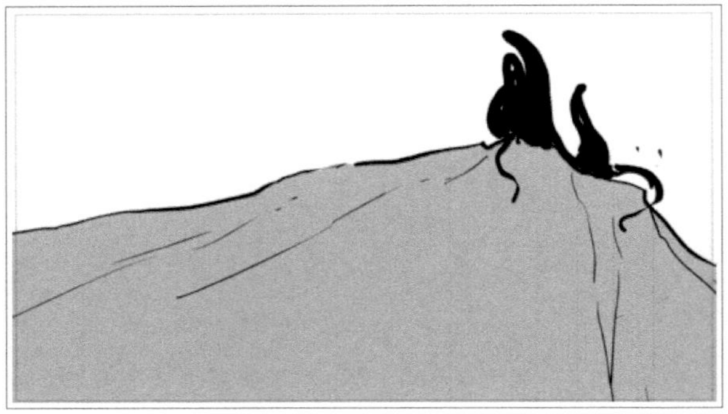

Scene	Duration	Panel	Duration
3	05:00	5	01:00

Scene	Duration	Panel	Duration
5	01:00	1	01:00

Dialog

BANQUO
What are these,
So withered, and so wild in their attire,

Action Notes

Down Shot
Banquo reacts. They stand with their swords drawn.

Scene	Duration	Panel	Duration
4	01:00	1	01:00

Dialog

BANQUO
That look not like th' inhabitants o' th' Earth
And yet are on 't?—

Action Notes

Wide Shot
Banquo and Macbeth speak to the Three Witches.

Scene	Duration	Panel	Duration
5	03:00	1	01:00

Dialog

BANQUO
Live you? Or are you aught
That man may question? You seem to understand
me
By each at once her choppy finger laying
Upon her skinny lips.

Action Notes

Over The Shoulder Shot
They sheath their swords as they speak to the Three Witches.

Scene	Duration	Panel	Duration
5	03:00	2	01:00

Dialog

BANQUO
You should be women,
And yet your beards forbid me to interpret
That you are so.

Scene	Duration	Panel	Duration
5	03:00	3	01:00

Dialog

MACBETH Speak if you can. What are you?

Scene	Duration	Panel	Duration
6	04:00	1	01:00

Action Notes

Medium Up Shot
The Three Witches rise and writhe as they hail Macbeth and Banquo.

Scene	Duration	Panel	Duration
6	04:00	2	01:00

Dialog

FIRST WITCH
All hail, Macbeth! Hail to thee, Thane of Glamis!

Scene	Duration	Panel	Duration
6	04:00	3	01:00

Dialog

SECOND WITCH
All hail, Macbeth! Hail to thee, Thane of Cawdor!

Scene	Duration	Panel	Duration
6	04:00	4	01:00

Dialog

THIRD WITCH
All hail, Macbeth, that shalt be king hereafter!

Scene	Duration	Panel	Duration
7	03:00	1	01:00

Dialog

BANQUO
 Good sir, why do you start and seem to fear
Things that do sound so fair?—

Action Notes

Medium Close Shot Zoom to Wide Shot as the Three Witches surround and envelope Banquo and Macbeth. The Three Witches swim around them as if they were floating in space.

Scene	Duration	Panel	Duration
7	03:00	2	01:00

Dialog

BANQUO
I' th' name of truth,
 Are you fantastical, or that indeed
BANQUO
 Which outwardly you show? My noble partner
 You greet with present grace and great prediction
 Of noble having and of royal hope,
That he seems rapt withal.

Scene	Duration	Panel	Duration
7	03:00	3	01:00

Dialog

BANQUO
I' th' name of truth,
 Are you fantastical, or that indeed
 BANQUO
Which outwardly you show? My noble partner
 You greet with present grace and great prediction
 Of noble having and of royal hope,
That he seems rapt withal.

Scene	Duration	Panel	Duration
8	11:00	1	01:00

Dialog

To me you speak not.
BANQUO
If you can look into the seeds of time
 And say which grain will grow and which will not,
 Speak, then, to me, who neither beg nor fear
 Your favors nor your hate.

Scene	Duration	Panel	Duration
8	11:00	2	01:00

Dialog

FIRST WITCH Hail!

Scene	Duration	Panel	Duration
8	11:00	3	01:00

Dialog

FIRST WITCH Hail!

Scene	Duration	Panel	Duration
8	11:00	4	01:00

Dialog

THIRD WITCH Hail!

Scene	Duration	Panel	Duration
8	11:00	5	01:00

Scene	Duration	Panel	Duration
8	11:00	6	01:00

Scene	Duration	Panel	Duration
8	11:00	7	01:00

Scene	Duration	Panel	Duration
8	11:00	8	01:00

Dialog

FIRST WITCH

Lesser than Macbeth and greater.

Scene	Duration	Panel	Duration
8	11:00	9	01:00

Dialog

SECOND WITCH

Not so happy, yet much happier.

Scene	Duration	Panel	Duration
8	11:00	10	01:00

Dialog

THIRD WITCH

Thou shalt get kings, though thou be none.

Scene	Duration	Panel	Duration
8	11:00	11	01:00

Scene	Duration	Panel	Duration
9	02:00	1	01:00

Dialog

THIRD WITCH
So all hail, Macbeth and Banquo!
FIRST WITCH
Banquo and Macbeth, all hail!

Action Notes

The Three Witches swirl around Banquo and Macbeth as they hail him.

Scene	Duration	Panel	Duration
9	02:00	2	01:00

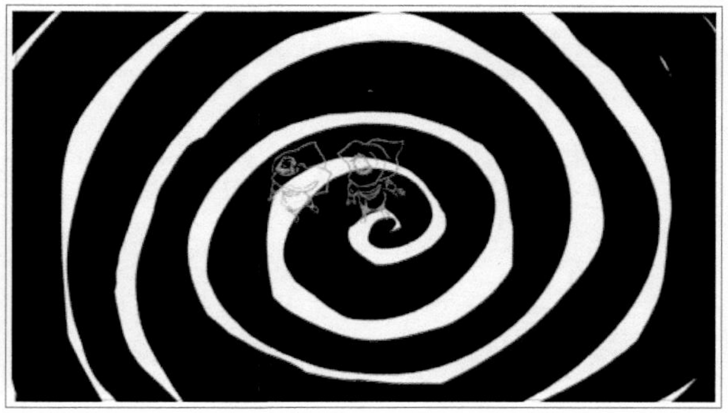

Dialog

THIRD WITCH
So all hail, Macbeth and Banquo!
FIRST WITCH
Banquo and Macbeth, all hail!

Scene	Duration	Panel	Duration
10	06:00	1	01:00

Dialog

MACBETH
Stay, you imperfect speakers. Tell me more.

Action Notes

Wide Shot to Medium Shot as Macbeth floats then walks towards the screen. The Three Witches cloud fades away and disappears.

Scene	Duration	Panel	Duration
10	06:00	2	01:00

Dialog

MACBETH
By Sinel's death I know I am Thane of Glamis.
But how of Cawdor? The Thane of Cawdor lives
A prosperous gentleman, and to be king
Stands not within the prospect of belief,
No more than to be Cawdor.

Scene	Duration	Panel	Duration
10	06:00	3	01:00

Dialog

MACBETH
Say from whence
You owe this strange intelligence or why
Upon this blasted heath you stop our way
With such prophetic greeting. Speak, I charge you.

Scene	Duration	Panel	Duration
10	06:00	4	01:00

Scene	Duration	Panel	Duration
10	06:00	5	01:00

Dialog

BANQUO

The earth hath bubbles, as the water has,
And these are of them. Whither are they vanished?

Scene	Duration	Panel	Duration
10	06:00	6	01:00

Dialog

MACBETH

Into the air, and what seemed corporal melted,

Scene	Duration	Panel	Duration
11	02:00	1	01:00

Dialog

MACBETH
As breath into the wind.
Would they had stayed!

Action Notes

Wide Shot
Banquo and Macbeth stand in en empty desolate landscape, the Three Witches are gone.

Scene	Duration	Panel	Duration
11	02:00	2	01:00

Dialog

MACBETH
As breath into the wind.
Would they had stayed!

Action Notes

Wide Shot
Banquo and Macbeth turn to walk back down the hill.

Scene	Duration	Panel	Duration
12	01:00	1	01:00

Dialog

BANQUO
Were such things here as we do speak about?
Or have we eaten on the insane root
That takes the reason prisoner?

Action Notes

Down Shot
Banquo and Macbeth trek down the hill, talking.

Scene	Duration	Panel	Duration
13	03:00	1	01:00

Dialog

MACBETH
Your children shall be kings.

Action Notes

Over the Shoulder Shot

Scene	Duration	Panel	Duration
13	03:00	2	01:00

Dialog

BANQUO You shall be king.

Action Notes

Over the Shoulder Shot to Medium Cowboy Shot
Banquo walks back to stand next to Macbeth

Scene	Duration	Panel	Duration
13	03:00	3	01:00

Dialog

BANQUO You shall be king.

With the understanding of all storyboarding fundamentals, you can take all these rules and basics and make your mark as a filmmaker. Watch films and learn to BREAK those rules sometimes… lots of the great filmmakers do and make great films in the process!

In this example, I use Macbeth again, where Macbeth hosts a dinner with colleagues, when the ghost of Banquo appears (only to Macbeth), to whom Macbeth argues and threatens. His guests look on in confusion…

In this scene, Macbeth's descent into madness can be staged in a variety of ways, hence breaking the rules…

Scene	Panel
1	1

Dialog

MACBETH I do forget.—
Do not muse at me, my most worthy friends.
I have a strange infirmity, which is nothing
To those that know me. Come, love and health
to
all.

Action Notes

Medium Wide Shot

Scene	Panel
1	2

Dialog

Come, love and health to
all.

Action Notes

Macbeth pleads with his audience.

Scene	Panel
1	3

Dialog

Then I'll sit down.—

Action Notes

He sits

Scene	Panel
1	4

Dialog

Give me some wine. Fill full.

Action Notes

He raises a glass to the steward.

Scene	Panel
2	1

Dialog

I drink to th' general joy o' th' whole table
And to our dear friend Banquo, whom we miss.
Would he were here! To all, and him we thirst,
And all to all.

Action Notes

Wide Shot

Scene	Panel
2	2

Dialog

LORDS Our duties, and the pledge.
⌜They raise their drinking cups.⌝

Scene	Panel
2	3

Dialog

LORDS Our duties, and the pledge.
⌜They raise their drinking cups.⌝

Action Notes

Macbeth reacts to seeing the ghost.

Scene	Panel
3	1

Dialog

MACBETH, ⌜to the Ghost⌝
Avaunt, and quit my sight! Let the earth hide thee.
Thy bones are marrowless; thy blood is cold;
Thou hast no speculation in those eyes
Which thou dost glare with.

Action Notes

Medium Shot

Scene	Panel
3	2

Dialog

LADY MACBETH Think of this, good peers,
But as a thing of custom. 'Tis no other;
Only it spoils the pleasure of the time.

Action Notes

Lady Macbeth pleads with her audience.

Note here! I choose to cross the 180 to convey chaos, confusion within Macbeth's mind….

Scene 4 | Panel 1

Dialog

MACBETH, ⌜to the Ghost⌝ What man dare, I dare.
Approach thou like the rugged Russian bear,
The armed rhinoceros, or th' Hyrcan tiger

Action Notes

Wide Shot

Scene 5 | Panel 1

Dialog

Take any shape but that, and my firm nerves
Shall never tremble. Or be alive again
And dare me to the desert with thy sword.

Action Notes

Close Up/ Macbeth looks SCREEN RIGHT.

Scene 5 | Panel 2

Dialog

Take any shape but that, and my firm nerves
Shall never tremble. Or be alive again
And dare me to the desert with thy sword.

Action Notes

Close Up/ Macbeth looks SCREEN LEFT.

In this shot, I twist the camera from a straight to a Dutch angle, again to convey his descent into madness.

Then quickly, I add a jump shot to convey the snap back to reality.

Scene	Panel
6	1

Dialog

If trembling I inhabit then, protest me
The baby of a girl. Hence, horrible shadow!
Unreal mock'ry, hence!

Action Notes

Zoom In to Dutch Angle

Scene	Panel
7	1

Dialog

Why so, being gone,
I am a man again.—

Scene	Panel
7	2

Dialog

Pray you sit still.

Action Notes

Jump Shot , back to reality

Last Words...

At the end of the day, you, the story artist, are visually interpreting a written story or script. Follow and understand the rules... and then see if you can break them and possibly create interesting and compelling shots that can define you as a unique filmmaker (think Steven Spielberg, Tim Burton, Akira Kurosawa, Guillermo del Toro, Christopher Nolan, John Frankenheimer, Michael Curtiz…)! Have fun doing visual illustrations, of your story, be prepared to draw and draw a lot. When you are storyboarding an animatic, you must be ready to animate your characters in key frames as they move from scene to scene. Understand that storyboarding is hard, but perhaps is one of the most rewarding work experiences ever especially when one sees one's contributions and work onscreen.

DOI: 10.1201/9781003599036-16

Index